Keep Paddling

Tommy Sewall

Keep Paddling
2017

JTS Publishing
ISBN: 978-0-578-19350-2

Printed in the United States of America

Cover photo: Jake Ingle

Contents

Chapter 1

The Otter Slide

It was a sunny mid-April day. We slid the raft into the river and quickly got set in our places. Nick and Zach were in the front of the raft, Nick on the left and Zach on the right. In the back, it was Cody and me. I was in the back right, where the guide sits, and Cody opposite me on the left. Our paddles dipped into the water as we paddled away from the rippling waters of the eddy and out into the water.

We were at the head of the Indian River. The Indian is a tributary of the mighty Hudson River, a premier whitewater river. At this time of the year, the water level on the Indian was too low to raft with any real success; but every day at 10:00 AM they opened the dam at the head of the Indian creating a "bubble" in the water level which made the river runnable for a window of time.

It was about 9:55 AM as we paddled out into the center of the calm water. We found a shallow spot in the river about thirty yards from where the first rapid began; we stopped the raft there while we waited for the dam to open and the water to rise.

Around sixty yards ahead of us was The Otter Slide. The Otter Slide is a raging, swirling rapid at the beginning of the Indian River. Most people choose to put their rafts and kayaks in the water just past The Otter Slide, but we saw the raging water flowing down the Otter Slide as a challenge to be conquered.

In fact, just a week before our trip we took the hour drive just to check out the notorious rapid. It is not a long rapid by any means. Most of the rapids we would face that day would be anywhere from seventy-five yards long all the way to the "mile-long-rapid." The Otter Slide is barely longer than 100 feet, but it drops steeply and has some intense waves and currents that make it extremely difficult. It's narrow, stuck between two cliffs, so there is not much room for error. It would be a challenge to make it through The Otter Slide unscathed, but if there is one thing we all knew, it was that we had to try.

> The Otter Slide is barely longer than 100 feet, but it drops steeply and has some intense waves and currents that make it extremely difficult. It's narrow, stuck between two cliffs, so there is not much room for error.

Now before we get into the particulars of what happened on that Class V Rapid, it's important for you to know some more of the details. You see, our whitewater rafting experience that day was much different than a typical rafting experience. When most people go whitewater rafting, they sign up at a whitewater adventure center (or someplace like that), they pay for the trip and are outfitted with all the right gear: life jacket, helmet, wetsuit, and paddle. Then a trained and certified whitewater rafting guide takes the group up to a river where they get into a giant raft. One of these rafts usually holds six or eight, maybe even ten people. They put it into the river, and the guide directs them down the river, steering them around all the hazards and taking them safely to the end.

Our experience was not like this. We had a 4-man raft. It's small. Think of the difference between a car tire running over a little bump in the road and a shopping cart wheel going over that same bump. We were in a "shopping-cart-wheel"size raft, it's significantly more intense.

On top of that, there was no one handing out gear, or helping us pick out helmets. Among the four of us, we had snowboard helmets, wakeboard helmets, and whitewater helmets. One time, on an earlier rafting trip, Zach was complaining about how cold his hand was getting. It wasn't until half way down the river that we realized he was wearing a fleece glove, which was literally soaking up the frigid water and making his hand go numb. Needless to say, we didn't have the nice matching helmets and paddles that the big rafts have; we had a pile of random gear scraped from wherever we could find it.

The biggest thing we were missing, however, was a guide. I was sitting in the guide's spot on the raft, and I could steer us pretty well, but half of steering is knowing where and where not to steer, and for that, I had no clue. I had rafted the Hudson before but had paid little attention to how to navigate the raging rapids.

We were as green as you could be. Our gear was hardly adequate, our experience was next to nothing, but our desire for adventure was off the charts.

Also with us that day was our friend Eric; he was planning on spending the day in his whitewater kayak leading us down the river. He chose to opt out of hitting The Otter Slide and instead stood on the shore filming the action with his cell phone. He had helped us scout the rapid out ahead of our launch. We had picked a line that we felt gave us the best chance of making it through without incident.

To the right side of the rapid was a dangerous cave where the water could easily trap a swimmer inside, so we knew we had to avoid that. On the left side, the water was a little smoother, it didn't have any caves to get trapped in, but it had a large rock that stuck out into the river, one that would be impossible to paddle around once we hit the fast moving water. We decided we needed to run the rapid in the center and aim for the left side just squeezing past the outlying rock face. To help us keep our bearings, we picked a boulder that was sticking out of the water close to the center of the river as our marker. Once we arrived there, we would have a good chance of hitting our projected path to safety. We just forgot one important thing: the water was going to rise over a foot before we hit the rapid.

As we waited anxiously for the dam to open and the water level to increase, we discussed our excitement and apprehension about running this rapid. We rehearsed the plan out loud; we went over the procedures for if you fall out.

- Keep your feet up (So they don't get caught in between two rocks causing you to get stuck underwater).
- Don't panic (It's always best to stay calm and control your breathing).
- Swim to shore (Pick someplace where the others in the raft would be able to pick you up).

As we waited, each of us holding a foot over the side of the raft on the river bed, we felt the river start to inch up our leg, telling us the water level was coming up. It became harder and harder to hold the raft as the shallow spot in the river quickly become deep.

I can remember Nick looking back at me from the front of the raft with a giant grin on his face.

He knew.

I knew.

We all knew.

The time had come.

We had spent all week preparing for what was just ahead of us, sitting in our offices daydreaming about what was about to come. Little did we know just how intense it would be.

We had already been rafting that spring at least four times. Just down the road from the town where we all lived and worked was a fun section of the Schroon River. It didn't offer any particularly hard challenges as it was mostly Class II and III rapids and, if the water was especially high, one Class IV. But each spring as the snow melted from the mountains, it flooded the Schroon, and if we hustled, we could leave our offices at 4:00 PM, and be done rafting before 6:30.

Let me take a moment to explain the class system; it's really pretty easy to understand.

> Class I is the easiest, mostly just fast-moving water with small ripples and waves.

> Class II is next, this one obviously has slightly bigger waves and small rapids but all easily navigable by a novice paddler.

> Class III is intermediate rapids, which require more skill. Guides are often needed in Class III rapid.

> Class IV is "intense, powerful, but predictable." ("International Scale of River Difficulty") Someone who falls out of his raft or kayak would likely need help getting out of this rapid.

> Class V is for Experts. "Extremely long, obstructed, or very violent rapids which expose a paddler to above average endangerment." ("International Scale of River Difficulty") Group rescue is almost a guarantee for this level rapid.

> Class VI is the highest rating, and it is the most dangerous and challenging. Americanwhitewater.org says "The consequences of errors are very severe and rescue may

be impossible." These are the rapids reserved for the best of the best. ("International Scale of River Difficulty")

We had spent some time practicing on the Schroon River getting used to the Class II and III rapids and also hitting the one Class IV that Schroon has to offer. We thought we were prepared and practiced to take on the Class V Otter Slide; we were wrong.

As 10:00 AM approached and the dam opened, the water began to rise, it picked up our feet, and the raft began to move. We locked into our positions on the raft. There were one or two good-sized waves that we would have to navigate before we got to the heart of The Otter Slide rapid.

> It didn't take me long to realize that the water had swallowed the rock that we had decided to use as a point of reference, so I steered the raft down the left side and yelled for everyone to paddle.

As the "guide", my job is to steer the raft with a longer, wider paddle that I use as a rudder, and also to control who is paddling by yelling out commands. For example, to move left in the river I would yell out "Right side paddle, Left side hold," and that would steer us to the left. Once we are pointed in the right direction, I would say something like "All forward," and off we'd go.

I began yelling out the commands and steering the raft towards the raging rapids. It didn't take me long to realize that the water had swallowed the rock that we had decided to use as a point of reference, so I steered the raft down the left side and yelled out for everyone to paddle.

In no time we entered the raging waters of The Otter Slide. We went shooting down and then blasted into a furious wave which launched our raft up into the air. Zach, whose section of the raft hit the wave the hardest, came flying out of his seat and slammed into Nick, immediately knocking them both into the surging water. This sudden imbalance of weight in the raft sent Cody and I reeling backward as the raft was tossed down the remainder of the rapid. Both Cody and I felt like we were riding a mechanical bull while we tried to stay in the raft, but all of the water rushing into the raft proved to be too much and we both fell out of the raft backward into the spinning rapid.

At that point, everything started to get blurry. My heart was pounding through my chest; the water, only in the 40s, immediately took my breath away. The spinning and fuming water caused instant disorientation. I was tempted to panic, but I remembered the rules of survival: feet up, don't panic, and swim to shore. I timed my breaths as I was still being pushed under water while being carried downstream.

Cody was just feet away from me.

I reached the shore and crawled up the river bank. I could see that Cody was almost to shore also. I had no clue where Nick was: I had not seen him since we capsized. I was

> Cody and I felt like we were riding a mechanical bull while we tried to stay in the raft, but all of the water rushing into the raft proved to be too much and we both fell out of the raft backward into the spinning rapid.

pretty sure Zach was right behind me in the river. As I pulled myself up, I looked back, and sure enough, there was Zach. He was down on all fours with drool or snot dripping from his face. I am still not sure which it was. He was white as a ghost and looked as though he was going to pass out. He looked up at me and said in an urgent yet grateful tone "I thought that was it." (That's a line we all still give him a hard time about to this day.)

When we went back and watched the video that Eric took from shore, Zach was underwater for hardly more than five seconds, but to him, it felt like an eternity. We all ended up just fine. Nick had ironically gotten tangled in the rescue rope, but it actually allowed him to get back to the raft and grab some of our paddles that were floating down the river. We lost one but had brought two extras with us just in case.

When we all finally met up fifty yards downstream, we enjoyed a good laugh and swapped our experiences of what had just happened. We dried off and gathered ourselves and prepared to set off for the rest of the day. As we got back in the raft and positioned ourselves for the rapids to come, Eric, who had watched from shore, and had more rafting experience than any of us, said, "Next time make sure you guys are **all** paddling when you hit a big rapid. You really have to 'punch through' the rapid if you want to stay in the raft."

He was absolutely right. When we went back and watched the video that he had taken, and the footage from the GoPro that we had with us in the raft, we hadn't **all** been paddling. Our friend Zach, riding in the front right of the raft and overcome with fear as we went flying down into the raging Otter Slide, had pulled his paddle out of the water and shifted his weight towards the inside of the raft. This had been the primary factor in our capsizing. (We still love to give Zach a hard time about this.) If he hadn't been so afraid and had kept paddling, we would have made it through The Otter Slide successfully.

It was, however, a lesson he learned quickly, and we kept reminding each other of it for the remaining five hours we were on the river that day. Every time we came to a section of big rapids I would yell out, "Paddle hard boys, we gotta' punch through it!" and we did. We worked as a team and paddled hard to make it through the rest of the rapids without falling out. We had a lot of fun that day. We made memories we will never forget, both scary ones and successful ones, but the lesson of the day goes much further than just rafting. It is a constant reminder to us in life.

The point of all of this is much greater than telling a funny story or preparing you for a whitewater rafting trip; it's about surviving the rapids of life. I want to describe to you an analogy, one that we will look at for the remainder of this book.

In this analogy the raft represents our faith; the relationship we have with the Creator of the universe and his Son, Jesus who gave His life so that we could survive the river of life.

The river is a picture of our life. It starts, when we are born, and we are on it until the day we die. There will be smooth and peaceful sections along the river of life that have breathtaking scenery and magnificent moments, but there are also going to be sections of the river of life that have rough whitewater. You know, just like the rapids I described in The Otter slide; foaming water swirling around sharp rocks jutting out of the turbulent water.

These times of troubled water are inevitable, no matter the length of the calm water, or how hard you work to avoid the whitewater, there will always be times in our lives when everything is trying to overwhelm and drown us. Without a raft, these whitewater difficulties are practically un-survivable, but with a raft, they can be navigated and conquered.

In this analogy the raft represents our faith: the relationship that we have with the Creator of the universe and his Son, Jesus, who sacrificed his life so that we could survive the river of life. As Christians, people who follow the teachings of Jesus and the Bible, we can have victory through the rapids of life. We do not have to settle for being tossed and flung at the mercy of the river.

Before I continue with the analogy, I feel as though I should clarify a point. The Bible is very clear about the requirements for a relationship with God. It is *"by grace, through faith,"* it says in the book of Ephesians, *"not by works."* The only way we can know God personally is by putting our trust in what Jesus did for us on the cross. If we try to add works to it, we are suggesting that His sacrifice was insufficient.

I am going to talk about some works, and how they play a role in helping us stay close to Jesus, or "in the raft," but I don't want there to be any confusion. The things that we do after we have a relationship with Jesus are all about keeping us close to him. The works that I will talk about help us to maintain our relationship with Jesus. Sometimes people make poor choices, believe the devil's lies, and end up walking away from their faith. If they actually trusted in Christ then nothing can permanently separate them again. The works that we will discuss in the

> The things we do after we have a relationship with Jesus are all about keeping us close to him.

next couple chapters are all about helping us stay close to Jesus and resting in his protection and plan, not about earning salvation or "staying saved".

"Keep paddling," the advice from our friend Eric, resonated with us for the rest of that day and even now. That is how you stay in the raft on the river, and that is how you keep your faith on the river of life. The blade of the paddle has two sides, and for the sake of this analogy pretend with me that one side of the blade says "The Bible" and the other side says "The Church." These two things will represent the paddle. Just like the paddle is the key to successfully navigating the rapids of the river, these two elements will be equally important to us as we navigate the rapids of life.

Without the paddle, it's only a matter of time before a rapid big enough to toss you out of the raft will come. Likewise, regardless of where you are in your walk with Christ, if you stop going to church and reading the Bible it's only a matter of time until something comes up that pushes you far away from Jesus. Thus, I want to take the next two chapters and show you what I mean, and encourage you to *keep paddling.*

Works Cited:

Walbridge,Charlie - Safety Chairman & Singleton, Mark – Executive Director American Whitewater, from "Safety Code of American Whitewater," Adopted 1959, revised 2005, Web 1 June 2017

Keep Paddling

Chapter 2

Paddle Side 1- The Bible

The *Word of God*, *Scriptures*, *The Holy Bible* - all different names for the book we most commonly call the Bible. This section is not meant to teach you the Bible, but rather to help you understand why the Bible is vitally important to your life.

That being said, I do think it's important to mention, the reason we give this book such power in our lives is that we believe it is literally God's words to us. He used many different authors to write his message to us. In 2 Peter 1 verses 20-21 it says *"Most of all, you must understand this: No prophecy in the Scriptures ever comes from the prophet's own interpretation. No prophecy ever came from what a person wanted to say, but people led by the Holy Spirit spoke words from God."*

This is an important piece to understand why the Bible is so important to our lives. It is not like other self-help books or pieces of literature. The content of this book is written by God, and not just the concepts, but the literal words are from the Almighty Creator of the universe. That is what separates this book out from the others and puts it on a special level that deserves such undivided attention. When we read this book, we are reading God's word. When we change because of this book, we are changing because of God.

While many thousands of pages have been written about the importance of the scriptures, I want to talk about just two particular passages; the first to help us better understand the value the Bible has for us, and the second to look at an analogy that the Bible uses to talk about its importance to us.

> The content of this book is written by God, and not just the concepts, but the literal words are from the Almighty Creator of the universe. That is what separates this book out from the others and puts it on a special level that deserves such undivided attention.

So, let's start with 2 Timothy 3:16. This is the Apostle Paul writing to the young pastor, Timothy. He says this about the value the Bible has on our lives:

"All Scripture is inspired by God and is useful for teaching, for showing people what is wrong in their lives, for correcting faults, and for teaching how to live right. Using the Scriptures, the person who serves God will be capable, having all that is needed to do every good work."

These two verses lay out pretty plainly for us the way that the Bible is meant to work in our lives. It's a book that teaches us. Its content is intended to grow our knowledge.

Paul continues on to show us specifically how it can teach us. First, it shows us things in our lives that we are not doing right. As we read it, and our knowledge of Jesus and how we should live our lives grows, it exposes areas in our lives that we had previously been operating in error.

Similar to many other areas of our life, we start with a very basic understanding of how something works or how to perform a particular task, and as we go through life, we encounter people who show us a better way or the right way. That is what the Bible does for us, it *corrects faults*. This phrase is a crucial phrase. It conveys that the Bible does not simply "show" us what is wrong, but it "corrects" us, it shows us the right way. If all it did were show us how wrong we are it would not be nearly as helpful, but that is what God wants us to know here, the Bible exposes **and** corrects.

If the verse ended there, we would be in trouble because that would mean the Bible would only help us once we have actually done something wrong, but the verse continues: for *teaching how to live right.* This means that the Bible can help us learn before we have even made a mistake or ventured off into an unknown. We can look to the Bible to enlighten us for things that are ahead, not simply things that we have already done.

The only question then is to what extent does the Bible prepare us? Paul answers it in the next phrase, saying that for someone who desires to serve God, the Bible will provide us with **all** that we need. This is also an important piece of the puzzle for us. If the Bible didn't offer us everything we needed to grow and to change, we would be left to search out other resources for how to serve God, which would be tough and confusing. Fortunately, though, that is not the case, God has written everything we need for life and godliness in the Bible.

There are other resources available to us, and many of them are great. Godly authors help us understand, but none of them are of such importance that honoring God with our life would be impossible without them.

So, it's important for us to read the Bible because it teaches us, and its lessons are complete. A student of the Bible will have **all** that he or she needs for life.

Secondly, as we look at the importance of the scriptures in our life, I want to show you a beautiful landscape scene described in the book of Psalms. It's found in the very first chapter.

David, the man who defeated Goliath and was king of the nation of Israel, paints a picturesque scene of a tree planted on the bank of a river, it's roots sinking deep into the fertile earth on the edge of a flowing stream. He describes the tree as being fruitful, and its leaves well-watered.

I love to look at satellite images of a desert plain; you can quickly spot any bodies of water or streams because the trees change from a dry brown to lush, green foliage. The trees that are close to the water supply are growing and flourishing; they have a much better chance of surviving the storms of life. David uses this image to help us see the benefit to staying plugged into the Bible. He says that if we "*delight in the law of the Lord*" (Psalm 1:2) we will be like this tree. When we spend time reading it, day and night, we will have the growth and strength of a tree planted on the edge of a river. For us to survive the rapids of life, we have to make reading the Bible a priority in our daily schedule. Just like the strong, healthy tree, drinking water every day, we must drink deeply from the Bible daily.

If you are a tree planted without access to water, you will dry up and die; if you are in a raft on a raging river without a paddle, you will fall out; and if you are trying to walk with Jesus without reading the Bible, you will fall away.

Chapter 3

Paddle Side 2- The Church

The other side of the paddle represents the Church. Much like the first side of the paddle, plenty can be said about the church, and countless studies that have been done. This section is not meant to be an exhaustive look at the doctrines of the church, but an encouragement to you to be a part of the church.

Paul uses a fascinating analogy to teach us about church involvement. He tells us that being a part of the church is like being a part of the body. Specifically, he talks about it being Christ's body. We are followers of Jesus when we are involved in the church, effectively acting as Christ in the way that we encourage each other and influence the world. Inside of this analogy, we have the local body, which would be the group of believers that we meet regularly within our own geographical area, and there is the universal body, which would represent all Christians around the world.

By getting plugged into our local body, we help the universal body influence the world. The problem arises when we stop being involved in the church and separate from the body. Paul says that as Christians, we each represent a different "part" of the body. When we are involved and participating with the body, then it is like your eye showing your foot where to step. They work together, each doing a different job, but to the same end.

By comparison, when we are not involved with the church, we are like an eyeball that is not connected to anything. We are not helping our feet watch where to step, or telling our head to duck under a low hanging branch; disconnected from the body, an eye is as good as a discarded grape, just waiting to be squished.

Each of us has unique things that we have been gifted with -- talents, and abilities that God has given us. He has a specific plan for us to use those as a part of his body. When we aren't plugged in and involved in the church, our gifts are not being used. It's an important part of our faith to engage with other believers.

Secondly, I want to connect the church back to our first point, the importance of reading the Bible. This is really a big part of why it's important for us to be involved with the church: it helps to keep us reading the Bible.

> Each of us has unique things that we have been gifted with-- talents, and abilities that God has given us. He has a specific plan for us to use those as a part of his body.

As we discussed earlier, the Bible is key to our goal of "staying in the raft," and one of the main reasons we need to be a part of a local church, the body of Christ, is to keep us connected to the Bible. This happens in several ways. First, the pastor should be sharing weekly from the Bible. If your pastor is not reading from the Bible every week, then you should look for a different church. The Bible is absolutely the key to our faith and to avoid using it is not acceptable. Listening to someone who has spent hours and hours studying it is one of the primary objectives to attending and being involved in church.

Secondly, when we are with fellow Christians, we should be encouraged to study the Bible because we can see how it has influenced and changed their lives.

As we go through rough sections on the river, our arms get tired, and we are tempted to take a break from paddling, but this is a costly mistake. When I look across the raft to see my friends, in equal amount of pain, still paddling, it encourages me to dig my paddle back into the water and push on. Likewise, as we go to down the river of life, things pop up and distract us, or maybe we go through a hard time of poor health, it can be tempting to let our daily study of the scriptures fall by the wayside. When we attend church and see how the Bible is helping others, and how it's encouraging, teaching, and correcting them, we are reminded of its importance.

Other times we might get to a part of the Bible that we have a hard time understanding. If we are plugged into the church, we have access to many other believers who might have more knowledge of that portion of the Bible than we do, or maybe they have been through some experiences in their life that have helped them to understand it better. The list goes on and on with ways that being involved in the body of Christ helps us in our daily discipline and pursuit of the spending time in the Bible.

Finally, let me wrap up this chapter with this thought. I have had young people tell me, "Well you don't understand, my church doesn't have cool people," or "It's all adults at my church, I don't get anything out of it." Maybe an excuse like that has been rattling around in your brain while you read this section about the importance of the church. You are probably right about the first part, I don't understand. I don't know your individual issues, or what you like or don't like, **but** I know that God knows every single detail. He loves you so much that he died for you, and he has you where you are for a reason. He hasn't made a mistake or messed up. The Bible tells us that *"His ways are higher than our ways."* (Isaiah 55:9) In other words, he does stuff that we don't always understand, but we can trust that he has a plan and that it's the best one for us.

I also know that the Bible does not specifically say, "Be involved in your local church **if** there is a cool youth group." It simply says be a part of the body. My suggestion to you is to be a part of the body of Christ that is local to you - - no matter what. Just remember what I said before, your pastor needs to be preaching from the Bible and not adding anything to it. If you have a Bible-believing local church, you should attend it and get involved with all your heart. God has not forgotten about you. He has a plan for you. Try it out, and ask God to help you feel connected to the body of believers He has placed in your life.

Chapter 4

The Importance of a Guide

    Whitewater rafting has become one of my favorite springtime activities, and I have also found it to be rich in illustrations that parallel our spiritual journeys. I wanted to conclude with some of those other lessons, not necessarily tied into the main example, but fun nonetheless.

    If you can remember back to the beginning of this book I talked about how our rafting experience was different because we were going on our own, we did not have a professional rafting company that we were tagging along with. We knew the reputation that the Hudson River had, but our excitement had convinced us that we could handle it. The first hour or so on the river was pretty basic except the aforementioned Otter Slide; we had no trouble navigating the whitewater. It was not until we entered the famous Hudson Gorge that we started to doubt our previous decision to run the river without someone guiding us.

    We had pulled off at a nice sunny spot on the river bank to eat a small snack and rest before entering the next three-hour stretch of the most demanding whitewater any of us had ever navigated. That is when Sandy and a friend paddled by in their Whitewater Kayaks. As they paddled by, we waved to them and called them over to the shore. They came over, and we talked with them for quite a while, asking them about their experience on the Hudson River. We quickly learned that Sandy was a whitewater rafting guide for one of the companies that operate on the Hudson. She was showing her friend, in the other kayak, the ropes of navigating the different rapids.

Once we realized her experience, we asked her for some pointers on how to hit some of the more challenging rapids ahead. After a few more minutes of talking, she agreed to go with us and offer us the best routes through each of the rapids. We were so relieved to have such a knowledgeable person to take advice from. She was very helpful, stopping with us above each rapid to give us the best line down through it. Saying things like, "On this rapid, the trick is to start river middle and then when you pass the big rock on your right, paddle hard to the left, so you miss the big hole in the center."

It was information that was invaluable to us. Otherwise, we would have just paddled blindly down each rapid, but with Sandy's help and knowledge, which she undoubtedly received from other guides who had taught her, and from making some of these mistakes herself, she helped us to avoid the dangerous spots in the rapids and have the best experience possible.

As we came to the end of that turbulent section of the river, we thanked Sandy over and over again and waved goodbye as she and her friend paddled on ahead. We, of course, were pulling off to rest and eat more snacks. For the remainder of the day as we paddled down to our take-out location we talked over and over again about how thankful we were that we ran into Sandy and that she had agreed to help us out. Who knows what would have happened if we had not had her knowledge to help us navigate the water that day.

That story actually gives us a pretty cool lesson for life. I am sure that many of you, as you read this find yourself in similar situations. Maybe like us, you are staring down some pretty big unknowns. You are hoping for the best, but concerned about how much you really didn't know, just like us. But on that day the difference was made by someone who was little older and had a lot more experience, and that can make a huge difference for you too.

If the writer of the book of Hebrews were writing the Bible about whitewater rafting, he would have probably said something like this, "Remember the rafting guides who taught you the way down the rapids. Remember how they paddled and how they finished, and copy their technique." Instead, though, the writer of Hebrews was talking to us about how to live the Christian life, and he said this, "Remember your leaders who taught God's message to you. Remember how they lived and died, and copy their faith" (Hebrews 13:7).

As we go through life, there will be times when we are unsure of the "waters" ahead. The Bible reminds us that when we are unsure of the way to take, that we can look to those who have gone before us; those who have studied the Bible longer than us; those who have "paddled those waters before." I love at the end of that verse how we are reminded to "copy their faith." We should try to imitate the way that they live.

As we go through life, there will be times when we are unsure of the "waters" ahead. The Bible reminds us that when we are unsure of the way to take, that we can look to those who have gone before us; those who have studied the Bible longer than us; those who have "paddled those waters before." I love at the end of that verse how we are reminded to "copy their faith." We should try to imitate the way that they live.

It's important to mention though that not everyone is qualified to be copied. Just like not everyone is qualified to give advice on how to navigate the Hudson River. If Sandy had started giving advice that was contrary to things we knew to be true already, then we would probably have hesitated to listen and heed her advice. Or if in our initial conversation we discovered that this was also her first time down the river then that would have made any advice she gave less vital. In the same way, as we go through this life and look for people to imitate or copy, we want to look for individuals who are knowledgeable about the Bible, and whose advice is always consistent with what the Bible teaches. Just like how we sort of "interviewed" Sandy before we trusted her advice, you too can do a little interview before you start to copy someone's faith. Ask them about their life experiences and how they make decisions; listen for how the Bible and the church influenced them. Ask them for some advice moving forward and again see if the Bible seems to be their main guide If it is, then they are someone who is probably worth copying. If their experience lacks the influence of the Scriptures and the church, or if they are living contrary to Biblical truths, then they are probably not a person you should consider imitating.

Take a few moments to think if you have anyone in your life right now who you can ask to help guide you. Make finding someone a top priority in your life.

One of the biggest mistakes we made the day we met the Otter Slide, was setting off down the river without anyone to help us. Fortunately, Sandy came along before we hit the longer, more difficult stretch of rapids, but you can learn from our mistake and find someone early on who can give you advice for all the "rapids" you will experience in life. It just might make the difference between you staying in the raft or swimming for your life.

Chapter 5

"Paddles Up!"

"Paddles up!" When we hear this call, we all take our paddles out of the water, raise them straight up into the sky and touch them together, echoing the call of "paddles up." Usually, there is some hooting and hollering that goes along with it. It's a celebration tradition among rafters, and we love doing it. We always do it at the beginning of the day on the water, and then before a particularly hard rapid, and then always after we conquer a difficult section of whitewater. It's a fun tradition and one of the best parts of any trip on a river. I wanted to end with this illustration because I think it is vitally important as we think back on all of the lessons of this book.

As we travel down the river of life, we know we will encounter times of great difficulty. Sometimes it may feel like we might not make it out alive. There may be some sections of life that roar with such overwhelming volume that we just want to stop the raft and get out. We might even wonder why we ever thought this trip was a good idea, but because of the strength we have in Christ, and because of the community of believers we have around us, these challenges can be navigated **and** celebrated.

When we are rafting, and we see a particularly hard section coming up, like "The Ledges," on the Schroon River, which is one of our favorite hits, we almost always put our "paddles up" before we hit it. We know that once we hit that rapid, there is a real danger and most of us have experienced the fear that comes with being thrown out of the raft on that rapid. But we put our 'paddles up' to calm our nerves and to focus our minds. It reminds us that we are a team and that we can get through this if we all work together.

Then after we make it through the rapid, we always celebrate with our "paddles up." We look back at the roaring water that we just conquered, and celebrate. Even though in the middle of the rapid, we felt like we might flip the raft or be thrown out, we made it out the other side, and we look back with grins on our faces as if to tell the raging river, "not that time!"

> God is and will always be victorious, He never wants us to fail. He will never allow us to endure a temptation that we cannot endure, He loves infinitely. It is because of these truths that we can look to the sky and yell "paddles up" ahead of any situation.

It is important for us to spend time celebrating the battles and the victories that we face in this life. As we look *ahead* at times of trial, we can celebrate with our fellow believers because we know that God has a plan. God is and will always be victorious, He never wants us to fail or to fall out, He will never allow us to endure a temptation that we cannot endure, He loves infinitely. It is because of these truths that we can look to the sky and yell "paddles up" ahead of any situation.

Likewise, we should do the same at the *end* of the trial. At the season in our life when we come out the other side we can look back, and we can see the faithfulness of God, we can recognize his plan and his provision for us. We can still see the rocks, eddies, and caves that Satan had hoped to use to topple us out of our raft, but we cling firmly to our raft and keep paddling. We smile knowing that our God won the battle and in Him we have victory. We shout "paddles up" with our friends and family and celebrate the faithfulness of God.

Jesus gave His life that we may experience the **"abundant life" (John 10:10).** That's the kind of life promised to us as we ride down the river of life! It is not a life of gloom and despair but rather one of adventure, and ultimately one of victory.

Keep paddling, find a guide or two to help, and don't forget to yell "paddles up" along the way.

For the record:

1. Zach is our good friend and does a great job whenever he goes rafting with us. We enjoy teasing him about his mistake that led to our 'demise' that day on The Otter Slide but he is an excellent whitewater paddler, and it's always fun to have him in the raft.

2. If this book has stirred your personal sense of adventure and you want to experience some whitewater first hand, <u>I highly suggest going with a professional rafting company</u>. You know the ones I described in the book that have matching helmets and paddles and most importantly, a professional guide. Then if you decide that you like the sport, you can think about getting your own raft. I <u>do not</u> recommend just setting out and learning the way we learned.

3. You can actually watch what happened on the famous Otter Slide, as the footage that our friend Eric took that day on his cell phone is on YouTube. You can watch it here-
https://www.youtube.com/user/tsewall

4. You can follow our rafting adventures and more on my social media pages. Both Twitter and Instagram are the same @tsewall.

www.ingramcontent.com/pod-product-compliance
Lightning Source LLC
Chambersburg PA
CBHW030011040426
42337CB00012BA/730